ANCIENT GREECE

IN **30** SECONDS

CATH SENKER

ILLUSTRATED BY ESSI KIMPIMÄKI
CONSULTANT: DR. MATTHEW NICHOLLS

IVY KIDS

Contents

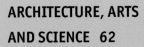

About this book
...in 60 seconds

Ancient Greece was one of the greatest civilizations of the ancient world. It is sometimes called 'the birthplace of Western civilization' because so much of Western art, architecture, science, political thought and literature comes from the trailblazing Ancient Greeks.

Ancient Greece was formed of the Greek mainland and hundreds of islands in the Aegean and Ionian seas in the Mediterranean. There were also Greek cities in modern-day Turkey, Sicily, southern Italy, parts of the Black Sea and even as far away as the south of France. The Ancient Greeks thrived from around 800 BCE to 30 BCE.

What do you already know about this civilization? You've probably heard that the ruins of Ancient Greek temples can be seen in modern Greece. Perhaps you know that the Greeks invented democracy – the system of government in most countries today. Greek thinkers came up with many basic principles in maths and science, too. The legacy of Ancient Greece is part of your daily life – you might go to the gym (a shortened version of the Greek word gymnasium) for exercise or work on a maths problem using pi (π). When you watch the Sun set, you know that Earth goes around the Sun, not the other way round – a discovery first made by the Ancient Greeks.

How do we know about the Ancient Greeks? They left behind a vast amount of evidence of their civilization. Some of their buildings survive, along with sculptures and statues. Archaeologists have excavated Ancient Greek cities and found thousands of beautiful vases, bowls and pots, decorated with scenes of daily life. Examples of Greek writing, which were carved in stone, have also been uncovered. Although many Ancient Greek books have been lost, copies of Greek works were made by the Romans and later, the Arabs, so Greek ideas survived.

This book reveals some of the details of life in Ancient Greece. You can find out about Greek homes – how did people stay cool in the hot climate, and how did they go to the toilet? Was their food healthy or horrible? How did they make a living, and what did they do for entertainment? How did they fight their battles or treat the injured and sick? You'll discover answers to these questions and many more.

Each topic has a page to read in 30 seconds. If you are in a hurry, simply read the 3-second sum-up. Every full-page illustration provides a colourful at-a-glance guide, too. If you have a few minutes to spare, check out the fact panels or have a go at the hands-on activities. You'll soon have a good grasp of life in Ancient Greece.

Ancient Greek society

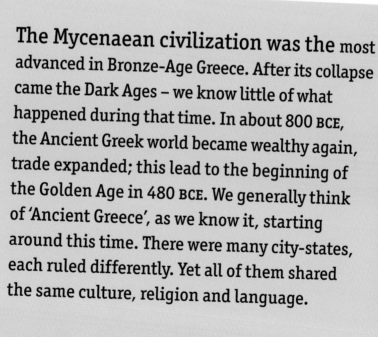

The Mycenaean civilization was the most advanced in Bronze-Age Greece. After its collapse came the Dark Ages – we know little of what happened during that time. In about 800 BCE, the Ancient Greek world became wealthy again, trade expanded; this lead to the beginning of the Golden Age in 480 BCE. We generally think of 'Ancient Greece', as we know it, starting around this time. There were many city-states, each ruled differently. Yet all of them shared the same culture, religion and language.

Ancient Greek society
Glossary

aristocracy The ruling class.

Asia Minor A peninsula of land in western Asia, bordered by the Black, Aegean and Mediterranean seas. The area forms part of modern-day Turkey.

BCE The abbreviation for 'Before the Common Era'. BCE refers to the years before the traditional birth year of Jesus Christ, while CE ('Common Era') refers to the years afterwards. Year 1 BCE is followed by Year 1 CE; there is no year zero between them. The terms 'BC' and 'AD' are sometimes used in place of BCE and CE.

citizen A free man born in his city-state. In Athens, citizens could vote in the Assembly and be elected to the ruling Council.

city-state A city and its surrounding area, which had its own laws, army and government.

civilization A society or group of people living together at a particular time and place.

colony An overseas settlement.

democracy A system of government in which citizens have a say in how they are ruled, including voting for their leaders and deciding on laws. The word democracy means 'rule by the people', from the Greek words demos ('people') and kratos ('rule').

export To take goods to a different part of the world to sell or trade.

fresco A wall painting done on wet plaster.

Golden Age The period of time from around 480 BCE to around 330 BCE, when Greek culture thrived, and great art, literature, philosophy and drama were produced. This time is also known as the 'Classical period'.

government A group of people who make and administer a country's or territory's laws.

hierarchy A system in which people or things are ranked according to their importance.

import To bring back goods from a different part of the world to sell.

oligarchy A system of government in which a small group of people are in charge.

papyrus Paper made from the papyrus plant, used as a surface for writing.

slave A man, woman or child who is owned by another person.

tyrant A powerful ruler of a city-state.

The Ancient Greeks emerge

... in 30 seconds

During the Bronze Age, from about 2500 BCE, the Minoan civilization developed on the island of Crete. The Minoans became rich by trading around the Mediterranean. Skilled craftspeople, they built a huge palace at Knossos, on Crete. Around 1500 BCE, volcanic eruptions and earthquakes changed the temperature and led to poor harvests. The Minoan civilization was weakened, making it easy for invaders to defeat them.

In c. 1600 BCE, another civilization, the Mycenaeans, arose on the mainland of what we now call Greece. The Mycenaeans took over Crete and the Minoan trade routes in the eastern Mediterranean. They spoke a form of Greek, and learned from the Minoans how to keep written records on clay tablets, many of which survive. Around 1100 BCE, tribes from the north overcame the Mycenaeans, and their civilization collapsed.

There is not much information about the Dark Ages that followed the Mycenaeans, since there were no written records of this period. It is known that local warlords took control of different areas, but life was probably little different for ordinary people, who farmed the land as always. The Greeks began to use iron instead of bronze to make tools and weapons. From around 800 BCE, the population became wealthier, and trade grew again. The Golden Age of Ancient Greece was about to begin.

3-second sum-up

The Minoans arose on Crete, followed by the Mycenaeans on the Greek mainland.

The palace at Knossos

At the heart of the ancient Minoan capital of Knossos was an impressive palace. It was decorated with beautiful frescoes and had its own water supply, indoor toilets and hundreds of rooms. The palace burnt down in around 1380 BCE and was not rebuilt, but you can still see its remains on Crete today.

The Minoans and the Mycenaeans were two great Bronze Age civilizations.

The Minoans (c.2500–1100 BCE) lived on the island of Crete.

The Minoans believed bulls were holy.

Minoan frescoes show men and women grabbing hold of a bull's horns and somersaulting over its back. It was all part of a religious ceremony.

Greece

Crete

Mycenaean civilization
Minoan civilization

The Mycenaeans (c.1600–1100 BCE) lived in small kingdoms all around the region.

The Mycenaeans recorded all goods that arrived in their cities on clay tablets.

Archaeologists have worked out how to read Mycenaean writing. They call it 'Linear B'.

The Greek city-states
... in 30 seconds

Ancient Greece in the Golden Age was not one single country. It was formed of more than a hundred city-states – mini countries, separated by mountains or formed on islands. Each city-state included the city and the land surrounding it. Most city-states formed near the coast, where there was flat land that was easier for farming and getting around.

Athens was the most powerful city-state. It included a large area of land and became wealthy through trade. Other important city-states were Sparta, Corinth, Argos and Thebes.

Each city-state had its own government and capital. They were ruled in different ways. Sparta and many others were ruled by an oligarchy, a small group of powerful people. Sometimes, a tyrant (one powerful man) took over. Some tyrants ruled well. Peisistratos was an effective ruler of Athens in the mid-6th century BCE, who got things done. Other tyrants were less successful. In the late 6th century BCE, Athens turned to democracy (see page 20).

Even though they were ruled differently, all the Greeks spoke the same language and shared the same culture and religion. The Greeks had a strong identity. They nicknamed non-Greeks 'barbarians' because they thought the babble of their foreign languages sounded like 'bar-bar-bar'.

3-second sum-up

Many city-states sharing the same culture made up Ancient Greece.

Metics

Foreigners who came from outside the city-state to work or trade were called metics. In Athens, they made up about 40 per cent of the population. Usually from other city-states, metics spoke Greek and could succeed in business and even mix with the aristocrats. But they could never become citizens of their adopted city-state.

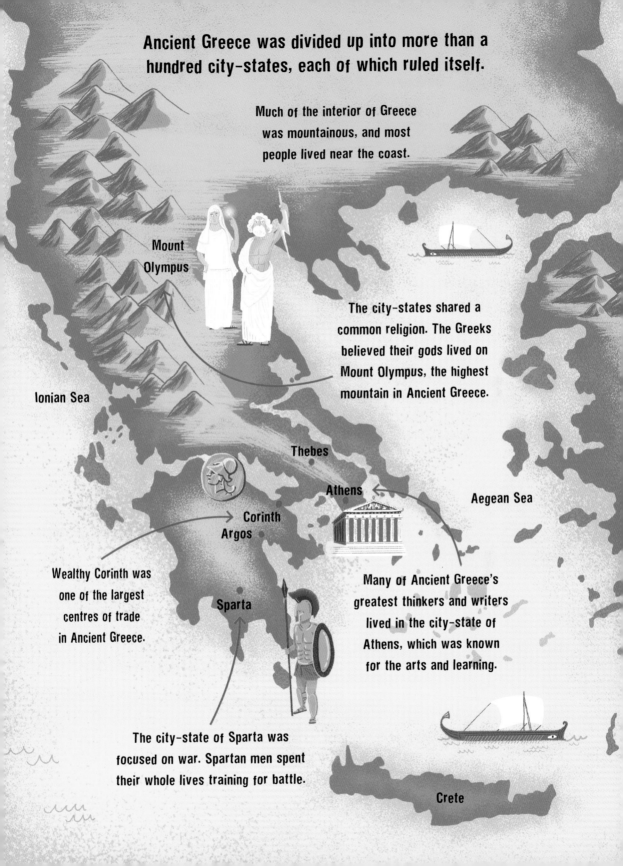

Ancient Greece was divided up into more than a hundred city-states, each of which ruled itself.

Much of the interior of Greece was mountainous, and most people lived near the coast.

Mount Olympus

The city-states shared a common religion. The Greeks believed their gods lived on Mount Olympus, the highest mountain in Ancient Greece.

Ionian Sea

Thebes

Athens

Aegean Sea

Corinth
Argos

Wealthy Corinth was one of the largest centres of trade in Ancient Greece.

Sparta

Many of Ancient Greece's greatest thinkers and writers lived in the city-state of Athens, which was known for the arts and learning.

The city-state of Sparta was focused on war. Spartan men spent their whole lives training for battle.

Crete

Off to the colonies
... in 30 seconds

Most ancient civilizations needed to be able to farm to grow their own food. However, with mountains covering around four-fifths of the mainland and some of the islands too, Ancient Greece had little space for agriculture. For this reason, adventurous young Greeks decided to form colonies in Asia Minor and around the Mediterranean.

The travellers sailed to modern-day Cyprus, Italy, Tunisia, Turkey and the east coast of Spain to settle. They risked storms at sea, shipwrecks and attacks by pirates to reach the new lands.

On arrival, they neither conquered the land nor drove out the local people, but set up colonies for farming. They also traded. Most people welcomed the Greeks, who sold them fine olive oil, wine, metal goods, pottery and cloth. In return, the Greeks bought grain, spices and salted fish, as well as papyrus, ivory, precious metals and wood. Grain was vital for feeding the people back in Greece. They also bought slaves – this terrible trade in human beings was normal in ancient times.

Greek identity was strengthened in the colonies because the settlers were far from home – they all missed Greek food and friends. The Greeks spread their lifestyle and culture to these lands.

3-second sum-up

The Greeks set up farming colonies in Asia Minor and the Mediterranean.

3-minute mission In a settler's shoes

It was difficult for Greek settlers to leave their country and everyone they knew behind. Imagine you are a young Greek adventurer heading off to one of the colonies. Write a letter to a friend about how it feels to go off to live in a new, unknown land. What will you miss, and what might you gain?

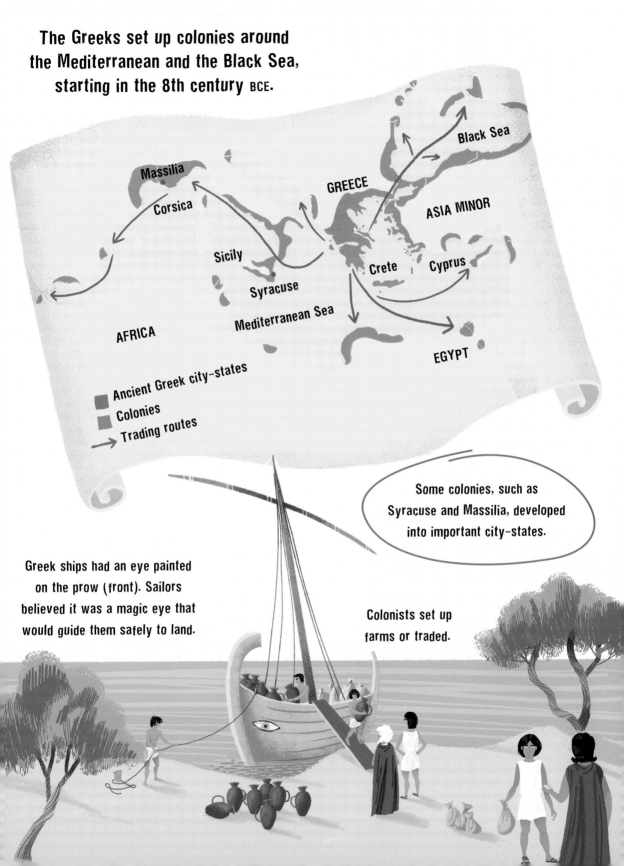

The Greeks set up colonies around the Mediterranean and the Black Sea, starting in the 8th century BCE.

Black Sea

Massilia

Corsica

GREECE

ASIA MINOR

Sicily

Crete

Cyprus

Syracuse

Mediterranean Sea

AFRICA

EGYPT

■ Ancient Greek city-states
■ Colonies
→ Trading routes

Some colonies, such as Syracuse and Massilia, developed into important city-states.

Greek ships had an eye painted on the prow (front). Sailors believed it was a magic eye that would guide them safely to land.

Colonists set up farms or traded.

Greek society

... in 30 seconds

In all the city-states, there was a hierarchy. At the top were the aristocrats; the rulers came from this group of citizens. Below them were the poorer citizens, who worked for a living. These people were mostly traders, craftspeople, labourers and farmers.

Women did not enjoy the same rights as men. They had to do as their father or husband said – this was part of Greek law. They could not play a full part in the public life of their city-state. For example, they could not hold political office or appear in court, and weren't allowed to buy or sell things above a certain value without permission.

At the bottom of society were the slaves. Some were captured in war, while others were born to slave parents or sold by people in desperate poverty to pay off their debts.

Many slaves worked in Greek homes – nearly every family had at least one slave. Some owners treated their slaves kindly and they became part of the family. Other masters beat or starved their slaves and forced them to work from dawn to dusk every day. These slaves usually died young. But even if a slave was well looked after, he or she had no freedom.

3-second sum-up

Ancient Greek society was made up of aristocrats, citizens and slaves.

The Laurion silver mines

The city-state of Athens owned the silver mines at Laurion, where up to 20,000 slaves and convicted criminals worked, in terrible conditions. The workers were sent down narrow shafts up to 100 m deep to dig out the precious metal. Producing silver goods helped to make Athens wealthy, but this didn't benefit the poor slaves.

Society in Ancient Greece was like a pyramid, with a few extremely wealthy people at the top and a mass of slaves at the base.

Aristocrats were the richest and most powerful citizens.
They had a comfortable life, with many slaves working for them.

A woman did not have the same rights as her husband.

Poorer citizens were free men who were born in their city-state.
They had to work for their living.

Craftsperson   Teacher   Farmer   Builder

Slaves were often defeated enemies. They had no freedom and could be bought and sold like goods.

Nearly half of the population of Ancient Greece were slaves.

Athens: rule by the people

... in 30 seconds

In Athens, at the end of the 6th century BCE, many citizens grew fed up of being ruled by the aristocracy. They wanted a say in government. In 508 BCE, a leading statesman, Cleisthenes, changed the way Athens was ruled. There would be no more oligarchies and tyrants. Instead, he set up the world's first democracy – a Greek word meaning 'rule by the people'.

All adult male citizens could take part in the Assembly, which decided on new laws. To make important decisions, at least 6,000 men had to attend the meetings, which were held once a month at a special place called the Pnyx. If there weren't enough people there, other citizens were dragged along from the streets! Everyone had the right to speak.

A Council of 500 citizens, chosen by lottery, put forward laws for the Assembly to discuss and ran the city-state's daily affairs. The Assembly also elected ten powerful strategoi (military generals), who commanded the army and navy. Even in modern democracies, citizens don't elect the generals.

However, most of the population were left out of Athenian democracy. The law gave men control over women, who had no individual rights. Metics were excluded too, as were slaves. Only a minority helped run Athens – but it was a start for democracy.

3-second sum-up

Under Athenian democracy, citizens had a say in how they were governed.

Ostracized!

The word 'ostracize' means to leave someone out of a social group – and it comes from Ancient Greek. The members of the Assembly had the power to vote to get rid of an unpopular politician. They scratched his name on a piece of broken pottery called an ostrakon. If enough people voted against one man, he was ostracized – exiled from Athens for ten years.

All male citizens of Athens could take part in the Assembly, which elected a Council and strategoi to run the city-state.

The Assembly made important decisions. It met every month at the Pnyx, on a hill above Athens.

The Assembly chose 500 men by lottery and appointed them to the Council. The Council ran the city-state's daily affairs. It met in the bouleterion (council house).

The Assembly elected 10 strategoi to run the army and navy.

Spartan life

... in 30 seconds

Athens' biggest rival was the city-state of Sparta. This was run by five powerful men called ephors and two kings. Sparta was a nation of warriors, and its army was considered the best in Ancient Greece.

The Spartans devised a cunning but unfair system to avoid doing the tough job of growing their own food. Sparta took control of the neighbouring state, Messenia, and forced the people to work on Spartan land. These unlucky labourers, known as helots, had to give half of the crops to their masters.

Although free from farming work, Spartan men were tied to the army for most of their lives. Girls went to school and learnt how to fight. It was thought that this would make them strong and ensure their babies were healthy. Boys were taken from their families when they were just seven to train as warriors. They were always left hungry and without enough clothes for the chilly mountain winter. The harsh conditions taught the boys how to survive in wartime by slyly stealing food and seeking shelter. There was even a thrashing contest each year to see who could take the most pain, and some died. Today we use word 'Spartan' to mean very strict, with no luxuries.

3-second sum-up

Spartan society was based on the army; all boys and men had to join.

Spartan women

In Sparta, women had more rights than other Greek women. They could own property and were even allowed to marry another man if their husband was away fighting for an extremely long time – although their new husband would have been a soldier too. With their husbands usually absent and no older children at home, there wasn't much family life for Spartan women.

The Spartans spent most of their lives training and preparing for war.

As children, girls and boys mixed together.

Boys left home at seven to live in an army boarding school, where they would practise sports and military drills.

Men became soldiers when they were 20 and stayed in the army for most of their lives.

Girls went to school to learn how to fight. They danced, ran, wrestled and threw javelins as part of their training.

Women ran the family farm and gave orders to the helots.

The helots grew all the Spartans' food for them. This left the Spartans with more time to fight.

Home life

We know a lot about the Ancient Greeks' daily lives, partly because some homes of wealthy people have survived. The Greeks had separate rooms for men and women, and a courtyard in the middle for outdoor living. Paintings on household objects show us what clothes people wore, which foods they ate, and how they stayed clean and healthy. Children led similar lives to their parents, but even poor children had some free time for toys and games.

Home life
Glossary

altar A raised structure or platform used for sacrifices to the Greek gods and goddesses, including Hestia, the goddess of the hearth and home.

BCE The abbreviation for 'Before the Common Era'. BCE refers to the years before the traditional birth year of Jesus Christ, while CE ('Common Era') refers to the years afterwards. Year 1 BCE is followed by Year 1 CE; there is no year zero between them. The terms 'BC' and 'AD' are sometimes used in place of BCE and CE.

citizen A free man born in his city-state. In Athens, citizens could vote in the Assembly and be elected to the ruling Council.

civilization A society or group of people living together at a particular time and place.

linen Probably the oldest kind of fabric, made from the grass-like fibres of the flax plant.

loincloth A single piece of cloth worn wrapped around the hips.

mosaic A picture or pattern made from small pieces of stone or ceramic.

slave A man, woman or child who is owned by another person.

At home with the Greeks

... in 30 seconds

Most Ancient Greeks lived in simple homes, with mud-brick walls. Some houses were made of stone, and have survived to this day. These homes probably belonged to rich people.

Men and women occupied different parts of the house. When men were home, they conducted business and entertained their friends in the andron, the men's area of the house. Women had their own space, the gynaeceum. Better-off women spent much of their time there, while slaves worked hard looking after the home and children. Poor women did all the housework and childcare themselves.

At least there weren't too many complicated cleaning tasks. Greek furnishings were basic. The floor was bare earth, although from the 300s BCE, wealthy people had attractive mosaics. Walls were sometimes plastered and painted red or white. People sat on couches or hard-backed chairs and ate food from low tables, which had three legs to balance on the uneven floor.

It was cool and dark indoors. Families spent most of the time outside in the courtyard, where the women cooked or sewed. The family altar was here too. In the warm Greek climate, the courtyard was the best place to be.

3-second sum-up

Greek homes were cool and dark with simple furnishings.

Going to the toilet

Only rich people had a bath and toilet at home, with running water linked to drains to take away the waste. Most people either shared an outside toilet or used chamber pots – like babies' potties. They simply emptied them in the street outside, so it was wise to be careful where you walked. The Greeks had no toilet paper; they made do with wiping themselves clean with stones.

Wealthy Greeks' houses were built of stone around a central courtyard.

Most Greeks lived in simple mud-brick houses, which crumbled away after a few years and had to be rebuilt.

In the gynaeceum, women wove, cared for the children, played games and chatted with their visitors.

Water for the bath was taken from the well and heated over a fire.

Small, high windows kept the building cool.

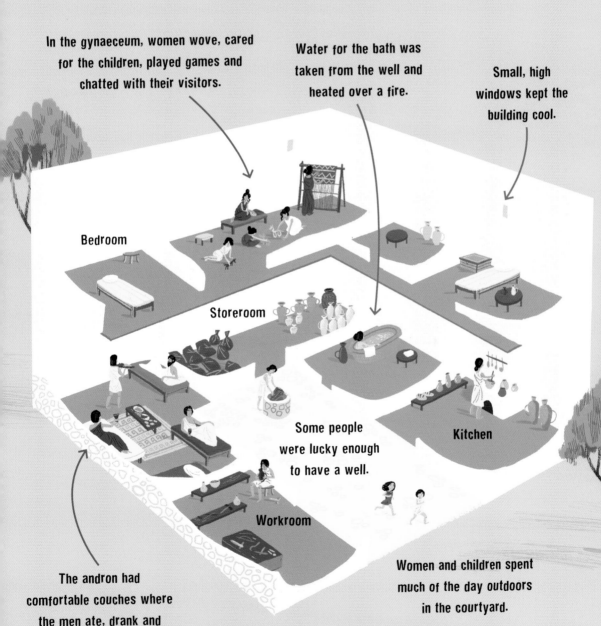

Bedroom

Storeroom

Some people were lucky enough to have a well.

Kitchen

Workroom

The andron had comfortable couches where the men ate, drank and talked with their friends.

Women and children spent much of the day outdoors in the courtyard.

Food and feasts

... in 30 seconds

In Ancient Greece, most people ate a simple but healthy diet, but wealthy people enjoyed stuffing themselves with a variety of rich foods at lavish feasts. Whether the meals were humble or extravagant, poor women and female slaves had the job of preparing them.

For breakfast, most people grabbed some barley bread soaked in wine or olive oil before heading to work. Lunch was a cold snack of bread with cheese, olives or fruit. In the evening, the Greeks sat down for a dinner of barley porridge and vegetables, and maybe some fish or eggs. Meat was rarely eaten.

The wealthy had feasts with all kinds of meat, from quails to snails, and game that they'd hunted: hares, deer or wild boar. Savoury or sweet sauces were added to the dishes. Rich people also loved fish and seafood – they ate fish on a bed of herbs, and octopus was very popular. For dessert, the tables groaned with fruit, nuts, cheese and honey cakes.

At mealtimes, the Greeks drank wine mixed with water; it was far too strong to drink on its own. Goats' milk was also commonly drunk. But hot drinks were off the menu in Ancient Greece – neither coffee nor tea were available.

3-second sum-up

Most people lived on bread, vegetables and fruit, and only the wealthy ate meat.

3-minute mission Make Greek pancakes

You need: 1 cup flour • 1 cup water • 2 tbsp honey • Olive oil • Frying pan • 1 tbsp sesame seeds • Adult helper

1 Mix the flour, water and 1 tbsp honey to make the batter.
2 Heat the oil and add a quarter of the batter. Cook the pancake until it is golden on both sides. Make three more pancakes.
3 Serve with the rest of the honey and the sesame seeds.

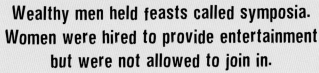

Wealthy men held feasts called symposia. Women were hired to provide entertainment but were not allowed to join in.

The diners played a silly game called kottabos, which involved flicking dregs of wine at a target.

The men ate with their fingers, scooping up food with flat bread.

Men reclined on couches while women or slaves served their food.

Sometimes, the party-goers ate and drank too much and were sick.

Female musicians played music and danced.

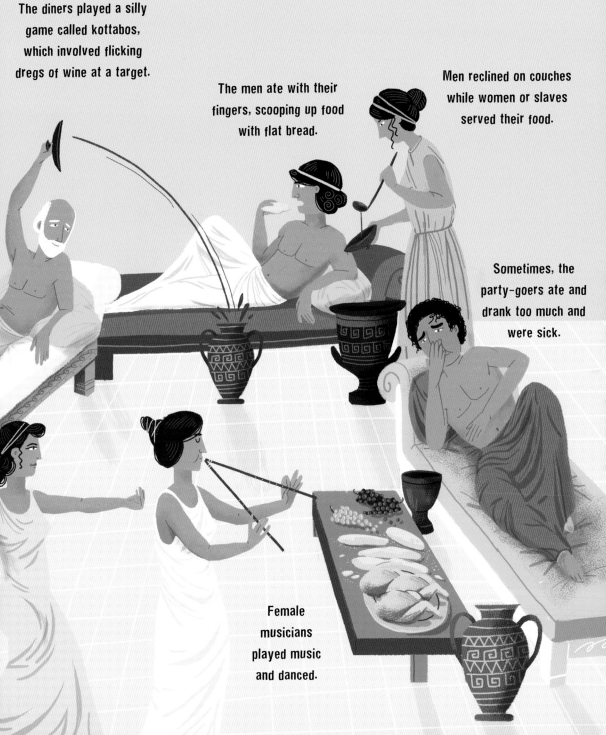

Greek clothes

... in 30 seconds

The Ancient Greeks kept their clothing simple. Most people wore a loose tunic, a single piece of cloth wrapped around the body and held in place with a brooch. Men wore knee-length tunics, while craft workers and slaves often just wore a loincloth. Women dressed in long tunics. The Ancient Greeks wore no underwear, so it was considered rude to lift up your clothing in public!

Ordinary people wore cream-coloured clothes (the natural colour of linen and wool). You could tell the rich apart because their tunics were made from soft silk and were often brightly coloured. They were dyed yellow with the spice saffron or purple from a kind of shellfish.

In cool weather, people wore a cloak called a himation over their tunic – another piece of cloth, wrapped around their body and thrown over the shoulder. Better-off people had leather sandals and shoes to protect their feet. The poor couldn't afford any footwear and went barefoot, even in winter.

Rich women loved to adorn their outfits with necklaces, earrings and bracelets from gold, silver or ivory. If you were poor, you had to make do with cheaper bronze, bone or glass jewellery.

3-second sum-up

The Greeks dressed in tunics, short for men and long for women.

Make-up

Greek women loved to wear make-up. They wore red or green eyeshadow, and smeared soot or charcoal on their eyebrows or eyelids. Women liked to appear pale as this showed they were wealthy and didn't need to work outdoors. They applied lead on their faces to make their skin whiter, but had no idea it was poisonous.

The chiton was the basic tunic worn by men and women from about 750 BCE to 30 BCE. They wore a linen or silk one in summer and swapped it for a woollen one in winter.

Most Ancient Greeks wore a simple tunic, with a warm cloak in cool weather.

Wealthy women had long hair to show they didn't have to work. They tied it up in elaborate hairstyles with ribbons.

There were no special garments for children; they wore smaller versions of their parents' outfits.

When it grew chilly, people wore a himation over their chiton.

People wore sandals outdoors but took them off in the house.

Health and healing
... in 30 seconds

Ancient Greek medicine was a mixture of magic and science. The early Greeks thought disease was a punishment from the gods, so treatments involved praying to Asclepius, the god of medicine, and offering him gifts. From the 400s BCE, doctors began to look to science to cure illness. The doctor Hippocrates taught medical students to examine patients and ask them questions to find out what was wrong.

Hippocrates also advised people to wash every day because staying clean helped to prevent sickness. The Greeks were the first civilization to provide public fountains with fresh spring water and bath houses with warm rooms and hot water.

Some Greek treatments were helpful. Doctors gave willow bark to reduce fever; a chemical found in this is still used as a painkiller today. Other treatments were unhelpful. Doctors thought that bleeding patients (letting out blood) could cure disease, but this made it worse. Bloodletting carried on until the 19th century and probably helped to kill many patients.

Surgery was extremely dangerous and best avoided. If the worst came to the worst, a doctor could cut off a diseased limb. But the patient would be lucky to survive the ordeal without dying of infection.

3-second sum-up

Greek doctors were able to cure some diseases but surgery was very dangerous.

Death and the afterlife

If they did not die of disease, many Greek citizens lived into their 60s. It was believed that the dead went to Hades, the Underworld. To reach it, they had to pay a ferryman to take them across the River Styx. At funerals, a coin was placed in the mouth of the dead person, to pay the ferryman. On arrival, heroes and good people went to Elysium, a happy place, while the wicked were sent to a horrible pit called Tartarus.

People bathed in cold water and then hot water to get really clean. Afterwards, they rubbed olive oil into their skin.

Hippocrates advised patients to rest and eat a healthy diet.

Many Ancient Greek treatments were helpful and based on common sense.

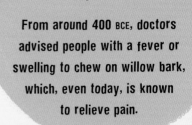

From around 400 BCE, doctors advised people with a fever or swelling to chew on willow bark, which, even today, is known to relieve pain.

Greek surgeons had the skills to set broken bones and pull teeth. Surgical instruments included scalpels for cutting flesh and retractors for pulling it back.

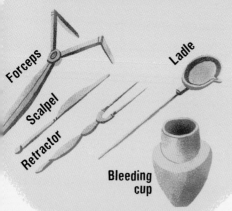

Forceps

Scalpel

Retractor

Ladle

Bleeding cup

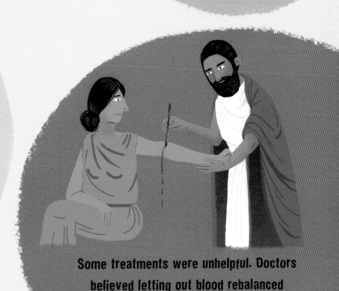

Some treatments were unhelpful. Doctors believed letting out blood rebalanced the body and cured disease.

Children: toil and toys

... in 30 seconds

Childhood was tough for poor children. They went out to work alongside their parents and did housework too. Even rich children were busy learning to follow in their parents' footsteps, although they probably had more free time.

Yet the Ancient Greeks were among the first peoples to see childhood as a separate stage of life. They allowed children the opportunity to play. Wealthy children enjoyed a range of games. They rolled hoops, romped on swings and seesaws, gave each other piggy backs and played leapfrog.

Children had toys too: spinning tops, rocking horses, little carts and boats, toy soldiers, animal figures and clay or rag dolls. They played board games similar to modern chess and draughts. The poorest children had home-made games including knucklebones, made from small animal bones.

Both boys and girls had the chance to play, but girls had a shorter childhood. At about 14, they had to give away their toys at the temple and were married to a friend or relative chosen by their father.

3-second sum-up

Wealthy children were given many toys and games while poor children made their own.

3-minute mission Play knucklebones

You need: Five small pebbles of a similar size

1 Using one hand, throw up your taw (the main playing pebble), pick up another pebble, and catch the taw on the back of your hand.
2 If successful, put down the pebble and use the taw to do the same again with each of the other pebbles in turn.
3 Play the same way, but this time pick up two pebbles at a time.
4 Next, pick up three pebbles together, then the final one.
5 Finally, pick up all four pebbles together.

Children played a variety of indoor and outdoor games.

Leapfrog was popular.

Knucklebones was a popular game (see opposite page). It was easy to find small animal bones on the ground and make a set.

Balls were made from a blown-up pig's bladder.

Dolls made from baked clay often had clothes carved on them and jointed arms and legs.

Just like today, small children enjoyed playing with wheeled toys.

Children ran along with hoops.

Education and work

For most of the Ancient Greek period, only boys were allowed to go to school, while girls stayed at home to help their mothers and learn how to run a household. Most people farmed for a living. Poor women worked alongside the men. Some people were craft workers, making household objects, tools, weapons and jewellery. At the market, traders sold their wares, and customers came to buy food and everything else they needed for the home – including slaves.

Education and work
Glossary

agora The central meeting place and main market area of a city, where citizens would come to meet, do business and buy and sell goods. The agora was surrounded by important government buildings.

amphora A jar with a narrow neck and two handles, which was used to store water, wine or oil.

BCE The abbreviation for 'Before the Common Era'. BCE refers to the years before the traditional birth year of Jesus Christ, while CE ('Common Era') refers to the years afterwards. Year 1 BCE is followed by Year 1 CE; there is no year zero between them. The terms 'BC' and 'AD' are sometimes used in place of BCE and CE.

city-state A city and its surrounding area, which had its own laws, army and government.

loom A frame used for weaving strands of thread or yarn into cloth.

military drill The training of soldiers for warfare, which included practising marching and learning how to use weapons.

spinning The process of changing fibres into yarn or thread. For example, fibres from the flax plant can be spun into linen yarn, ready to be woven into cloth.

stylus A metal 'pen' used for writing on a wax tablet.

41

Learning for life

... in 30 seconds

The Ancient Greeks believed the world of work was for men while a woman's place was in the home. Girls stayed in the house, where their mothers taught them how to run a household. For most of the Greek era, except in Sparta, only boys went to school.

Girls learnt cooking, weaving and clothes-making. In rich families, they sometimes had a home tutor to teach them to read, write and play an instrument. Playing music was seen as a suitable pastime for girls.

Parents had to pay for their sons to go to school, so only wealthy boys had a full education from age seven to eighteen. Poor boys only attended for three or four years, while the poorest couldn't afford to go at all. School subjects included maths, reading and writing, public speaking, poetry, music and sport. Children wrote on tablets – wooden boards coated with wax.

In Sparta, education was totally different from the other city-states. All boys were trained by the army. They learnt to read and write a little but mostly practised sports and military drills.

3-second sum-up

Boys were educated at school, while girls learnt how to run a household.

3-minute mission Make a simple wax tablet

You need: 2 pieces of A4-sized corrugated cardboard • Pencil • Ruler • Scissors • Glue • Wax • Bowl • Saucepan • Toothpick • Adult helper

1 On one piece of cardboard, draw a line 2 cm from the edge all the way round. Cut out the middle part to create a frame. Stick the frame onto the other piece of cardboard.

2 Ask an adult to put the wax in a bowl and place it over the saucepan, half filled with hot water. The wax will melt. Carefully pour a thin layer of wax onto the tablet. Once it has set, pour on another layer. Allow to set. Use a toothpick to write on your tablet.

Greek boys went to school, while girls stayed at home.

Sport was extremely important – the boys did lots of boxing, wrestling and running.

A slave called a paidagogus went to school with the boy and was allowed to beat him if he was naughty.

Maths was a major subject.

Children wrote on wax tablets. They scratched into the wax with a stylus and then smoothed it over for reuse.

Girls learnt how to run a household from their mothers.

They were taught spinning, clothes-making and cooking.

Some girls were lucky enough to have an education at home. They learnt how to read, write and play musical instruments.

Farming the land

... in 30 seconds

Many people relied on farming for a living but it was hard work. Olives and grapes grew well in the rocky soil of the hillsides, but there was little flat ground for crops. Most farms were small and produced just enough food for the family. Fortunately, the climate was good for growing crops, with hot, dry summers and cooler, wetter winters.

Olives were valued highly in ancient times, and people all around the Mediterranean happily exchanged goods for Greek olive oil. The Greeks loved their wine, too. A large part of the grape crop was turned into wine, but some grapes were kept for eating and drying to make raisins.

The main crop grown was barley – the grain was used for making bread. It was sown in autumn and grew over the rainy winter and spring. Farmers grew many kinds of fruits and vegetables, including apples, figs, peas, beans, lentils, onions and garlic. They grew flax to weave into linen.

Greek farmers also kept sheep for their wool, goats for their milk and hides, and pigs and chickens for their meat. Near the coast, many worked as fishermen, going out in small wooden boats to catch seafood and fish using nets and spears.

3-second sum-up

Farmers grew many crops and kept animals for their milk and meat.

3-minute mission Make raisins

You need: Fresh, undamaged grapes • Scissors • Slatted tray

1 Check the weather forecast is dry for the next three days.
2 Remove the large stems, leaving the small ones on the grapes. Wash the grapes well.
3 Place the grapes on the tray outdoors in a dry, sunny place. If you get dew overnight, bring them in.
4 After two to three days, you should have raisins!

Farmers harvested olives from November to March. It was a long and tiring job.

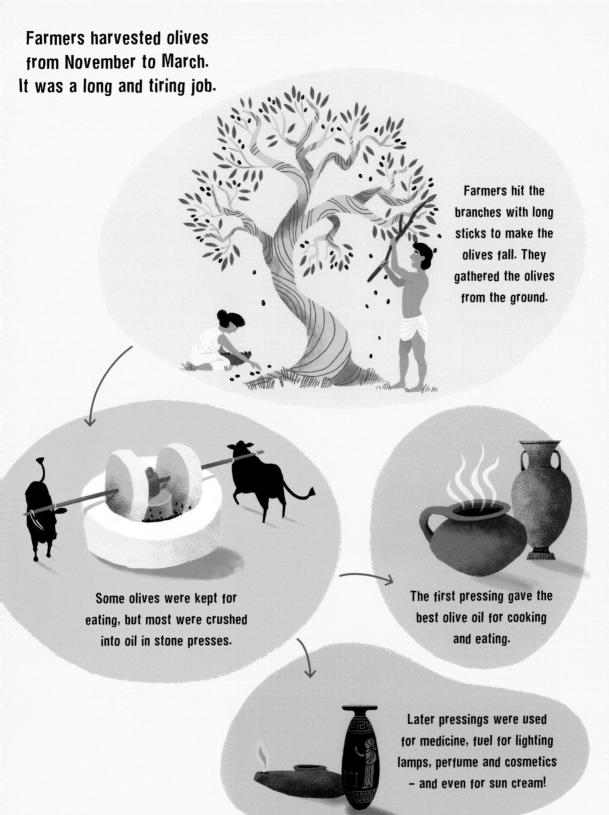

Farmers hit the branches with long sticks to make the olives fall. They gathered the olives from the ground.

Some olives were kept for eating, but most were crushed into oil in stone presses.

The first pressing gave the best olive oil for cooking and eating.

Later pressings were used for medicine, fuel for lighting lamps, perfume and cosmetics – and even for sun cream!

Creative crafts

... in 30 seconds

Women and girls were skilled craft workers, making all the family's clothes at home. At the market, craftspeople fashioned a wide variety of pots, crockery, shoes, bags and jewellery in their workshops.

Making clothes was a lengthy business – people had to make the cloth itself first! It is said that a woman called Pamphile on the island of Kos invented the technique of extracting silk fibre from moths to spin and weave into fine, luxurious silk cloth. Most women used cheaper wool or linen. They spun it into thread, wove the thread into cloth on a loom, and sometimes dyed it. From the cloth, women made all their family's outfits and home furnishings. Poor people sold woven products in the market for a bit of extra money.

Craftspeople made practical objects for daily use. They were proud of their work and wanted the items to look good. Athens was famous for its excellent black-figure (and later red-figure) pottery. Vases, plates and bowls were beautifully decorated with scenes from everyday life, such as farming and festivals.

The Greeks worked with metals too. Bronze was used for making weapons and amphoras – jugs for water, wine and oil. Corinth was famous for its fine silver and gold jewellery, which was popular with wealthy women.

3-second sum-up

Women made clothes, and other craftspeople produced crockery, weapons and jewellery.

3-minute mission Make a black-figure pot

You need: Terracotta pot • Pencil • Black acrylic paint

1 Decide on your design – look at images of black-figure pots online for inspiration.
2 Sketch your design on the pot in pencil.
3 Paint your design and allow it to dry.

Greek craft workers were famous for their fine cloth, beautiful pottery and metalwork.

Most women wove cloth, even rich ones. They used a vertical loom. Cloth was rolled up at the top as it was woven.

Black-figure pottery was made by painting pictures onto red clay pots using slip (watery clay) before firing. Detail was scratched into the black parts afterwards.

Skilled metalworkers made everything from weapons, bowls and drinking cups to fine jewellery.

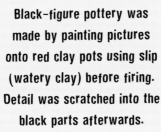

Pottery fashion changed in the late 6th century BCE. The background was painted with slip, leaving the pictures and patterns red – this was red-figure pottery.

Off to market

... in 30 seconds

The hub of every town was the agora – the local market.
People gathered here to buy and sell goods, exchange news and gossip. It was noisy and chaotic, with traders calling out to customers, and clowns and acrobats entertaining the market-day crowds.

In flat, coastal areas, there were roads, so traders could transport their wares to market in carts. But Greek roads were poorly made, full of potholes and gullies. Many people loaded up donkeys or mules with their goods and walked instead.

In the agora, people could buy everything from fruit to sheepskins and slaves. Most of the traders sold food. Craft workers sold their wares, and cobblers, barbers and blacksmiths offered their services. Slave traders brought their captives for local people to examine and purchase.

Before money was invented, goods were exchanged. If you wanted a goat, you might trade some of your chickens. Coins were probably invented at the end of the 7th century BCE in the city-state of Lydia, in modern-day Turkey, and spread around the Greek world. It made life easier because people could buy and sell without swapping goods directly. Every city-state made its own coins, usually showing a favourite god or goddess.

3-second sum-up

Food, household items and services were traded at the agora, which means 'place of open assembly'.

Law and order in the agora

The Greeks had standard weights and measures for wet and dry goods, and all traders had to use them. Inspectors called metronomoi went round checking that they did. There were also market police – the agoranomoi, who were in charge of enforcing the rules, stopping arguments and catching cheats.

The agora was the market in the middle of every Greek town.

Traders called out to passers-by to buy their wares.

In the open part of the agora, there were food stalls.

Rich women didn't leave the house much. Their husbands did the shopping.

Men could get their hair cut by the barber while they were out shopping.

Poor women shopped and traded at the agora. But Athenian women weren't allowed to buy or sell anything worth more than a small measure of barley.

Religion and festivals

Religion was central to the lives of the Ancient Greeks, and they believed in a wide range of gods and goddesses. As well as worshipping the gods at home, people came together at festivals to honour them at elaborate temples. Each temple was dedicated to a particular god or goddess. The Olympic Games emerged from a religious festival to worship Zeus. This five-day competition attracted contestants from all over Greece.

Religion and festivals
Glossary

altar A raised structure or platform used for sacrifices to the Greek gods and goddesses.

BCE The abbreviation for 'Before the Common Era'. BCE refers to the years before the traditional birth year of Jesus Christ, while CE ('Common Era') refers to the years afterwards. Year 1 BCE is followed by Year 1 CE; there is no year zero between them. The terms 'BC' and 'AD' are sometimes used in place of BCE and CE.

citizen A free man born in his city-state. In Athens, citizens could vote in the Assembly and be elected to the ruling Council.

city-state A city and its surrounding area which had its own laws, army and government.

colonnade A row of evenly-spaced columns, usually holding up a roof.

comedy A type of Greek play intended to make people laugh, involving singing, dancing, rude jokes and a happy ending.

frieze In Ancient Greek architecture, a frieze is a band of carved decoration around the top of a building. It comes above the columns and below the triangular pediment.

Golden Age The period of time from around 480 BCE to around 330 BCE, when Greek culture thrived, and great art, literature, philosophy and drama were produced. This time is also known as the 'Classical period'.

hoplite A Greek foot soldier.

priest/priestess A religious official who was responsible for a temple and the religious events connected to it. A priest or priestess would also perform animal sacrifices to the gods.

sculpture A three-dimensional (3-D) figure or design carved from stone, wood, clay or another material.

temple A building used for religious worship and ceremonies.

tragedy A type of Greek play that was very serious, with a sad ending and a moral lesson about right and wrong. Tragedies were often based on myths from the past.

Gods and goddesses

... in 30 seconds

The Ancient Greeks believed in many gods and goddesses. Rather like humans, the gods lived, loved and fought – but they never grew old or died. People thought that the gods had power over everything they did.

There were twelve main gods on Mount Olympus and many lesser ones. Zeus was the king, and the most powerful. One of his brothers, Poseidon, ruled the sea, and another brother, Hades, was the god of the Underworld. Zeus was married to Hera, the protector of women and marriage, but he was constantly unfaithful to her with mortal women. Zeus and Hera's son Ares was the god of war – he was savage and fierce, and always fighting.

The Greeks prayed to the gods every day at their altar at home, which was usually in the courtyard. The whole family worshipped together – even the slaves joined in. They said prayers, offered gifts of food and sacrificed small animals.

The Ancient Greeks thought that humans could make a bargain with the gods, making offerings in return for health and happiness. They would praise the gods and ask them to cure an illness, send a good harvest or bring victory in war.

3-second sum-up

The Greeks prayed to the gods to help them in their daily lives.

Advice from the oracle

The Greeks sought advice from the gods, especially over important decisions, such as whether to go to war. They visited a place called the oracle, made a sacrifice (often a goat) and asked their question. A priest or priestess acted as the go-between. At the oracle at Delphi, the god Apollo gave advice through a priestess called a Pythia. The Pythia inhaled the smoke of burning laurel leaves, went into a trance, and provided Apollo's response. It was usually vague, leading to big debates about its meaning.

ZEUS
King of the gods

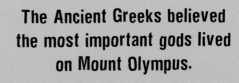

The Ancient Greeks believed
the most important gods lived
on Mount Olympus.

HERA
Wife of Zeus,
goddess
of marriage

APOLLO
God of the Sun,
medicine and
music

ARTEMIS
Goddess of
the Moon and
hunting

POSEIDON
God of the sea

HESTIA
Goddess of
the home

APHRODITE
Goddess of love

ARES
God of war

ATHENA
Goddess of wisdom
and war

HERMES
Messenger
of the gods

HADES
Ruler of the
kingdom
of the dead

DEMETER
Goddess of
agriculture

HEPHAESTUS
God of fire

Temples

... in 30 seconds

The Greeks provided a home for their gods on earth: a temple. The earliest temples were made of simple mud bricks and timber, but by the Golden Age, sturdy stone temples were found all over Greece. These temples were the most elaborate buildings of any city-state.

The Greeks believed the gods' spirits resided in the temples. Each temple was dedicated to a particular god or goddess and had a huge statue of that god. For instance, at Corinth the temple housed a statue of Apollo. When the doors to the temple were opened, the god looked out on to a large courtyard. At festivals, the whole community gathered to offer special gifts and honour him.

At temples, priests led the worship of gods, but it was often down to priestesses to lead the devotions to goddesses. In Athens, the Parthenon temple was dedicated to the goddess Athena, the guardian of the city. The Parthenon priestesses were seen as the vital link between the spiritual world and the people of Athens. Being a priestess was the most important job available to Greek women.

3-second sum-up

Beautiful temples were built for the worship of the Greek gods and goddesses.

The Elgin Marbles controversy

The Elgin Marbles are a collection of sculptures taken from the Parthenon and shipped to London by the British Lord Elgin in 1802–12. After an outcry in the UK over his greedy actions, the government bought the treasures and placed them in the British Museum. The Greek government wants the sculptures returned, but the British Museum argues it is protecting them for everyone. Read about this debate online, and decide whether you think the Elgin Marbles should stay in the UK or go back to Greece.

The Parthenon, built from 447 to 432 BCE,
was the most impressive temple in Athens
– and perhaps the whole of Greece.

The marble friezes around
the outside were decorated
with sculptures showing the
procession of worshippers
to the temple.

The Parthenon was on the Acropolis,
a high, flat area above the city where
all the temples were built.

The colonnade around the
edge of the temple had 8
columns on the two short
sides and 17 on the two long
sides. Many of these columns
are still standing today.

Many of the temple's sculptures
can be seen in museums across
Europe, mostly in Athens and the
British Museum in London, UK.

In the inner shrine
of the Parthenon was
a 12m-high statue of
the goddess Athena.

The wooden figure was covered
in precious ivory, and her dress
was made from pure beaten gold.

Festivals

... in 30 seconds

You might think the weekend feels too short so have pity for the poor Ancient Greeks, who had no weekends at all. Festivals were the only chance to have a few days off, so everyone looked forward to them. They gave wealthy women a rare opportunity to get out of the house, too. Everyone dressed up, men drank wine, and even slaves could have fun.

The Greeks held sports, harvest and religious festivals as well as celebrations for weddings and birthdays. Religious festivals were the biggest. The Panathenaia took place every year in Athens to celebrate Athena's birthday. Every four years the Great Panathenaia was held, lasting for six days.

The Panathenaia ended with a procession to the Parthenon to offer generous gifts and animal sacrifices to Athena. Bulls were led to the stone altar in front of her statue and their heads were pulled back to face the sky. The animals' throats were cut, blood gushed everywhere, and it is said that the women screamed! The Greeks believed that the gods liked the animals' fat and bones, which left the meat for the humans to enjoy.

3-second sum-up

Religious festivals were the most important special occasions in Ancient Greece.

The Festival of Dionysus

Dionysus was the god of wine, farming and theatre, so Dionysian festivals in Athens were devoted to drinking, feasting and enjoying plays. All citizens attended – probably women as well as men – as well as visitors from around Greece. A noisy procession of people singing and drinking wine carried a bronze statue of Dionysus through the streets to the theatre. For several days, the Athenians watched lengthy performances of tragedies and comedies, and at the end, the best playwright won a prize.

The Panathenaic festival celebrated Athena's birthday with a procession, animal sacrifices and feasting.

The most important citizens led the procession to the Parthenon.

A new golden-coloured woven dress was brought for Athena's statue.

Bulls were led to the temple and sacrificed. The meat was roasted over a fire on the altar and shared in a huge free feast for everyone.

Soldiers and priests took part, as well as dancers, musicians and poets.

Even slaves and women had some time off from their duties to enjoy the festival.

The Olympic Games
... in 30 seconds

The Greeks knew that sport helped to keep people fit and healthy, which they thought was especially important for soldiers. Sports were part of religious festivals. In Olympia from 776 BCE, sports contests at a festival to praise Zeus developed into the Olympic Games.

Held every four years, the Olympics were the greatest spectacle of the time. Armies even stopped fighting wars to allow athletes from all over Greece and thousands of spectators to travel to Olympia. A smaller contest for women called the Heraia also took place, with running races held in the same stadium but on a shorter track.

The Olympic Games were for men only. The athletes competed entirely naked, and married women were forbidden to watch; if a woman was caught, she was thrown off a mountain as punishment. Some events were similar to those held today, such as running, jumping and discus throwing. Others you wouldn't recognize.

The victorious athletes were adorned with a wreath of olive leaves. They returned home in glory and were treated as heroes. One of the best-known athletes was Milon of Croton. A wrestler, he won six victories at the Games in the late 6th century BCE.

3-second sum-up

Male athletes from all across Greece competed in the Olympic Games.

Origins of the marathon

In the days before the postal service, long-distance runners often relayed messages from one place to another. In 490 BCE, the Greeks defeated the Persians at the Battle of Marathon and sent a runner with the good news back to Athens – a distance of about 39 km (24 miles). This famous run is the origin of the marathon race, which took place for the first time in 1896, at the first modern Olympic Games. Today, the official marathon distance is just over 42 km (26 miles).

The Olympic Games were part of a religious festival to honour Zeus, the king of the gods. Local priests acted as judges of the contest.

The Games were only for men, and they competed naked.

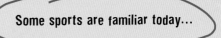

Some sports are familiar today...

Javelin throwing

Running

Long jump

Discus

Other sports are not so familiar...

In the hoplite race, runners wore leg armour and helmets, and carried a heavy shield.

A mixture of boxing and wrestling, the rough sport of pankration only ended when one fighter passed out. All tactics were allowed except for biting and gouging out eyes.

The four-horse chariot races were very dangerous, with 40 chariots hurtling around the track for the 14-km race.

Architecture, arts and science

Ancient Greece is well-known for its extraordinary art and architecture – lifelike statues and majestic public buildings with tall columns and intricately carved friezes. Just as famous are Greece's great thinkers, who met at the gymnasium not only to exercise but also to discuss philosophy, science and new inventions. For relaxation, the Greeks loved retelling myths and the stories of heroes. A favourite pastime was visiting the theatre to watch tragedies and comedies.

Architecture, arts and science
Glossary

archaeologist Someone who studies human life in the past, by looking at the objects ancient people left behind.

BCE The abbreviation for 'Before the Common Era'. BCE refers to the years before the traditional birth year of Jesus Christ, while CE ('Common Era') refers to the years afterwards. Year 1 BCE is followed by Year 1 CE; there is no year zero between them. The terms 'BC' and 'AD' are sometimes used in place of BCE and CE.

bust A sculpture of a person's head, shoulders and upper chest.

chorus A group of performers who describe and comment on a play, using song, dance and speeches. They often speak in unison (at the same time).

circumference The length of the edge around a circle.

city-state A city and its surrounding area which had its own laws, government and army.

diameter A straight line that passes through the centre of a circle, from one point on its circumference to another.

displace To move something from its usual position.

empirical Based on what you see or experience, rather than on theory and reasoning.

frieze In Ancient Greek architecture, a frieze is a band of carved decoration around the top of a building. It comes above the columns and below the **pediment**.

Golden Age The period of time from around 480 BCE to around 330 BCE, when Greek culture thrived, and great art, literature, philosophy and drama were produced. This time is also known as the 'Classical period'.

gymnasium A room or building used for exercise in Ancient Greece. It was also a place for socializing and discussing ideas.

kiln An oven used for firing (baking and hardening) clay sculptures and pots.

myth A traditional story that is not true, and often involves a hero, gods and goddesses, and supernatural events.

pediment A triangular section on the face of a building below the roof, above the entrance. It is often decorated with sculptures.

philosopher A person who discusses ideas about the meaning of life.

pi The ratio of a circle's circumference to its diameter, approximately equal to 3.14 and shown using the symbol π. The circumference (C) of a circle equals π multiplied by the diameter (D) – $C = \pi D$.

sculpture A three-dimensional (3-D) figure or design carved from stone, wood, clay or another material.

Trojan War A famous war between the Greeks and the Trojans in Greek mythology. It began when the Trojan prince Paris ran off with Helen, the wife of King Menelaus of Sparta. Menelaus and other Greek kings fought the Trojans for 10 years, and eventually defeated them.

volume The amount of three-dimensional (3-D) space occupied by a substance or object.

Sculptors and statues
... in 30 seconds

From the 7th century BCE, the Greeks made life-sized statues in marble, limestone or bronze to honour their gods and the heroes of the day. Many statues were naked – that's because the Greeks linked nudity to heroism. Sculptors used muscular athletes as models.

The sculptures from the early Greek period (660–480 BCE) were rather rigid and angular, and not particularly true to life. But during the Golden Age of Athenian culture (480–330 BCE), sculptures became more realistic. Artists had a better understanding of how the human body looked and moved, and they developed a greater range of expressions to show emotions.

The statues depicted gods, goddesses and the celebrities of the day – politicians and athletes. They all showed perfect humans: beautiful, graceful women and well-proportioned men. Some were so lifelike, it looked like they might breathe and move. Statues were brightly painted, with glass or stones added for eyes.

Few Greek sculptures have survived. Many limestone and marble statues were later burned and turned into lime, used to make cement, while those made from precious metal were melted down, and the metal was reused.

3-second sum-up

In the Golden Age, artists made lifelike sculptures of gods, athletes and politicians.

3-minute mission Carve a soap bust

You need: Internet access • Bar of soap • Toothpick • Butter knife

1 Choose an image of a Greek bust online.
2 Place the soap vertically. Carve the outline of the face, hair (or helmet) and neck on the soap with the toothpick.
3 Use the knife to carefully chip off the soap outside the outline.
4 With the toothpick, add detail to the face and create the hairstyle.

Artists used the 'lost-wax casting method' to make statues and other sculptures from bronze.

1. A finely detailed wax model was made over a rough clay core.

2. Layers of clay were applied to the wax model.

3. The model was baked in a kiln. The wax melted, leaving behind a clay mould with a narrow hollow space.

4. Molten metal was poured into the space. It cooled and hardened.

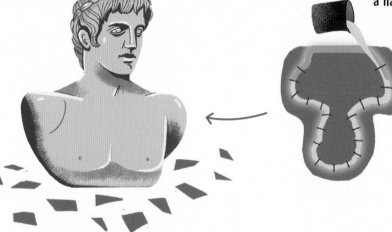

5. The clay shell and the rough clay core were broken away to reveal the hollow metal sculpture.

Stone statues were made from limestone or marble, and shaped using mallets and chisels.

Architecture

... in 30 seconds

Greek architects were famous for the careful and accurate design of their buildings. They calculated all the measurements and angles before construction started.

Most public buildings had columns. Horizontal beams were laid across the columns, with the roof over the top. This is classical Greek design. If you see a building like this today, you'll know that it was inspired by the Ancient Greeks.

By the 400s BCE, the towns in Greek city-states were planned in neat grids, with areas dedicated to different activities. Most towns had stone walls around them for protection. The main road from the city gate usually led to the agora, the large, square marketplace. Around it were stoae – covered walkways that protected people from the sun and the rain. The stoae were open on one side, and full of market stalls and shops.

Important government buildings were constructed near the agora. In Athens, the Council met in the bouleterion, a large room designed with tiers of seats on three sides so everyone could hear each other. The top Council committee met in its own round building, the tholos.

3-second sum-up

Greek cities and the buildings within them were carefully planned.

3-minute mission Design a Greek temple

You need: Internet access • Paper • Ruler • Pencil • Felt tips

You are a time-travelling architect and have been commissioned to build a new temple. Look online at Greek temples for inspiration, and then draw your own, using a ruler to make sure the measurements are accurate. Decide how many columns your temple will have, and how tall they will be. Will they be in Ionic, Doric or Corinthian style? Design the frieze and pediment that will be carved around the top.

Classical Greek-style buildings have columns, an architrave, a frieze and a pediment.

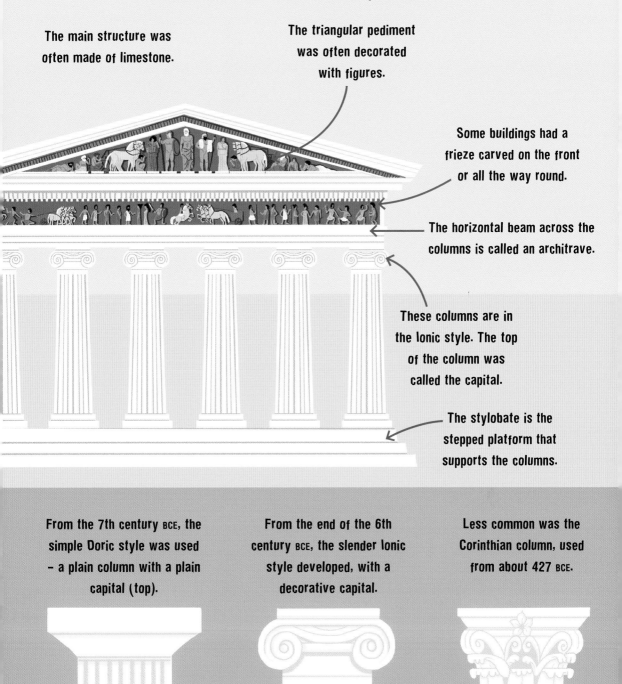

The main structure was often made of limestone.

The triangular pediment was often decorated with figures.

Some buildings had a frieze carved on the front or all the way round.

The horizontal beam across the columns is called an architrave.

These columns are in the Ionic style. The top of the column was called the capital.

The stylobate is the stepped platform that supports the columns.

From the 7th century BCE, the simple Doric style was used – a plain column with a plain capital (top).

From the end of the 6th century BCE, the slender Ionic style developed, with a decorative capital.

Less common was the Corinthian column, used from about 427 BCE.

Great thinkers
... in 30 seconds

Ancient Greek philosophers, including Socrates, Plato and Aristotle, came up with ideas that form the basis of modern Western philosophy.

The word 'philosopher' means 'lover of knowledge'. Philosophy is the study of human nature, knowledge and reason. Greek philosophers pondered the meaning of life – questions such as 'how do we know things exist?' They considered how people should behave and countries be governed.

Plato

Socrates (470?–399 BCE) thought that people should use reason to develop their ideas and work out truths. He asked lots of questions so that people could identify where their thinking was flawed. For example, he argued that he did not fear death because he did not know what followed. How could he fear something unknown? He encouraged his students to question everything too.

Plato (428?–348? BCE) was one of Socrates' students. He focused on morals – issues of right and wrong. He wrote a book called *The Republic*, about the best way to govern a city-state. Plato argued that philosophers should become kings or kings become philosophers, because philosophers were intelligent and wise. The most famous of Plato's students was Aristotle (384–322 BCE). He developed logic, the science of reasoning.

3-second sum-up

Greek philosophers discussed how people behave and how countries should be governed.

3-minute mission Think like a philosopher

Aristotle came up with the idea of syllogism, which has three parts. Here is an example:
All birds lay eggs. A swan is a bird. Therefore a swan lays eggs.
Can you think of your own example of a syllogism? Make sure that every sentence is correct, or your logic will be flawed.

Plato used this story about a cave to show that you cannot rely only on empirical knowledge – what you see and hear.

These prisoners have been kept in a cave and can only see the back of it. A fire reflects the shadow of people and animals that pass by. The prisoners think the shadows are real.

One prisoner escapes. She starts to realize that her former view of the world was wrong.

Wow! So what I thought was real wasn't real after all.

She returns to tell the prisoners about the real world, but they threaten to kill her if she sets them free.

But I'm telling you, the REAL world is out there!

We don't believe you. Go away!

The escaped prisoner stands for the philosopher, who seeks knowledge outside of the cave.

Science and inventions

... in 30 seconds

Greek philosophers loved to discuss mathematical and scientific ideas. They tried to work out how the world worked by searching for natural causes of events rather than accepting that they were the actions of the gods.

If you're learning about circles in maths, you can thank the great scientist Archimedes – in the 3rd century BCE, he worked out the value of pi. He is also famous for another important discovery. It's said that when he jumped into a full bathtub, he noticed how lots of water splashed out. He realized that by measuring the amount of water his body displaced, he could find its volume.

Around the same time, Aristarchus of Samos worked out that Earth moves around the Sun and even calculated the distance between them. But no one believed him – they still thought the Sun moved around Earth. His theory gained little support until the 16th century.

In around 1900 CE, a Roman shipwreck was discovered near the Greek island of Antikythera. Among the wreckage was a complicated device with up to 40 cogs and gears. It turned out to be an Ancient Greek machine for working out the movement of the stars and planets. It was the world's first computer – 2,000 years old!

3-second sum-up

Ancient Greek scientists made important discoveries in maths, science and astronomy.

3-minute mission Discover pi for yourself

You need: Circle of card • Piece of string • Scissors

1 Wind the string around the circumference of the card and cut it to that length.
2 Stretch the string across the diameter of the card, and cut as many string diameters as you can. You should be able to cut three diameters and have a little string left over. That's because pi = 3.14. The circumference is the diameter x 3.14.

Archimedes was a brilliant mathematician, astronomer and inventor.

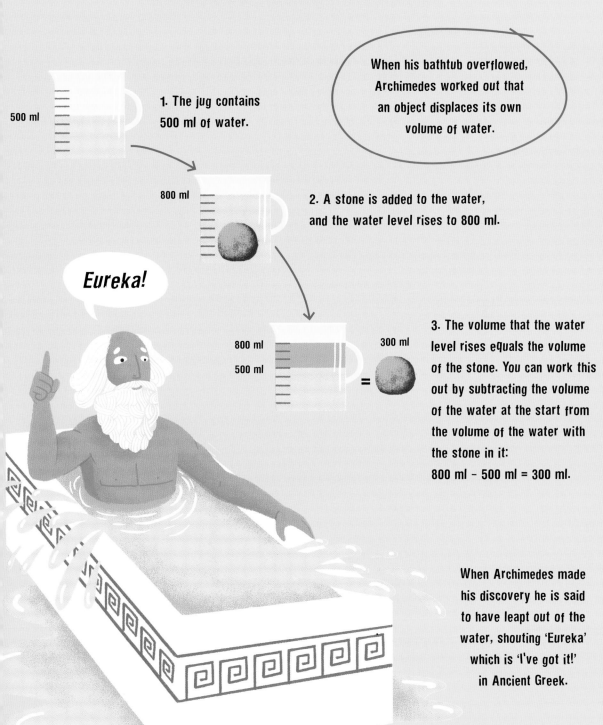

1. The jug contains 500 ml of water.

500 ml

When his bathtub overflowed, Archimedes worked out that an object displaces its own volume of water.

2. A stone is added to the water, and the water level rises to 800 ml.

800 ml

Eureka!

3. The volume that the water level rises equals the volume of the stone. You can work this out by subtracting the volume of the water at the start from the volume of the water with the stone in it:

800 ml – 500 ml = 300 ml.

800 ml
500 ml
300 ml

When Archimedes made his discovery he is said to have leapt out of the water, shouting 'Eureka' which is 'I've got it!' in Ancient Greek.

Superb storytellers

... in 30 seconds

The Greeks were fantastic storytellers. They created myths to explain the forces of nature they did not understand, such as the creation of the world, the sun moving across the sky and earthquakes. Poets recited the adventures of gods, heroes and monsters.

Here's how the Greeks accounted for the changing seasons. The god Hades fell in love with the harvest goddess Demeter's daughter, Persephone, and whisked her off to the Underworld. Demeter was so upset that she ruined all the crops. Hades compromised, and allowed Persephone to return to Earth for six months a year. While she was there, Demeter was happy: spring and summer arrived, and the crops grew. When Persephone went back to Hades, the season turned to autumn, then winter.

Poets told stories of the Greek heroes and their amazing adventures. The two greatest Greek poems are Homer's *Iliad* and *Odyssey*, possibly composed in the 8th or 7th century BCE. The *Iliad* is about the Greek war with Troy, while the *Odyssey* tells the story of the hero Odysseus on his journey home from war.

Around 600 BCE, the poet Sappho lived on the island of Lesbos, where women had more freedom than on the mainland. Sappho wrote about the loves and hates of wealthy women. Sadly, just one of her complete poems survives.

3-second sum-up

Poets told stories of heroes, and myths were used to explain natural events.

The Trojan War: fact or fiction?

The Greeks wrote down the history of real events as well as stories, and sometimes they were blended together. Parts of the story of the Trojan War are clearly invented – for example, gods and goddesses appear. Yet the tale is probably based on real events; archaeologists have found evidence of a city called Troy and battles in the area. So the story seems to be a mixture of fact and fiction.

The Greeks loved to tell stories of brave heroes.

The greatest Greek hero was Heracles. He carried out 12 extremely difficult tasks, which included killing a lion with his bare hands.

Perseus defeated the snake-haired Medusa, whose gaze turned people to stone. He used his shield as a mirror to avoid looking at her directly.

Odysseus outwitted the one-eyed Cyclops, who had imprisoned him and his men in a cave. The group blinded the Cyclops and escaped by clinging underneath his sheep as they left the cave to graze.

Theseus defeated the Minotaur, a monster that was half-man, half-bull.

At the theatre

... in 30 seconds

The Ancient Greeks loved going to the theatre. Plays were performed as part of religious festivals and went on for several days. The theatres were outdoors, and thousands of people attended.

Comedies and tragedies were the main types of plays. Comedies were full of slapstick humour and rude jokes. Tragedies were extremely sad – most of the characters met a grisly end. The best-known Ancient Greek playwrights include Euripides, Aeschylus and Sophocles, who wrote tragedies, while Aristophanes crafted comedies.

Euripides

Although many plays were about powerful women, all the actors were male. They dressed up to play female characters. The actors wore masks for the different characters, with expressions to show their emotions. They wore padded costumes, high shoes and wigs to make them visible even to the people right at the back. The lines were spoken or sung, to the accompaniment of music.

The majority of the audience were men, as women were discouraged from going out in public. If people didn't like the play they were watching, they chucked food at the actors. Ancient Greek theatre was a rowdy affair.

3-second sum-up

Theatre audiences adored watching comedies and tragedies.

3-minute mission Make a mask

You need: Paper plate • Pencil • Scissors • Hole punch • Elastic

1 Holding the plate to your face, mark the position of your eyes and mouth on the front.
2 Draw the expression you want, then cut out the eyes and mouth.
3 Punch two holes in the sides of the plate. Thread a length of elastic through, then secure with knots.

The actors wore masks so that the audience could see their expressions – happy, sad, delighted or furious.

Ancient Greek theatres had a huge, semi-circular seating area, a raised stage and an 'orchestra', an area where the chorus sang.

A hoist behind the stage lifted up actors so it appeared as if they were flying!

The seats were made of stone so it was best to bring a cushion to avoid a sore bottom.

In the orchestra, the chorus sang to explain what was going on.

War and the end of the Golden Age

Life in Ancient Greece was not always peaceful. The city-states had armies of trained warriors. They sometimes went to war against each other and at other times joined forces to defend Greece from outside invaders. In the 300s BCE, Alexander the Great from Macedonia, in northern Greece, conquered Ancient Greece and created a vast Macedonian empire. Yet Greek culture continued to spread. Even when the Romans took over in 30 BCE, they kept alive the Ancient Greek customs and lifestyle.

War and the end of the Golden Age

Glossary

Asia Minor A peninsula of land in western Asia, bordered by the Black, Aegean and Mediterranean seas. The area forms part of modern-day Turkey.

battering ram A large, heavy log used to batter and break down walls and gateways.

BCE The abbreviation for 'Before the Common Era'. BCE refers to the years before the traditional birth year of Jesus Christ, while CE ('Common Era') refers to the years afterwards. Year 1 BCE is followed by Year 1 CE; there is no year zero between them. The terms 'BC' and 'AD' are sometimes used in place of BCE and CE.

catapult A machine used for hurling rocks and other missiles through walls to attack a city.

citizen A free man born in his city-state. In Athens, citizens could vote in the Assembly and be elected to the ruling Council.

city-state A city and its surrounding area which had its own laws, army and government.

conscript To force someone to serve in the army.

democracy A system of government in which citizens have a say in how they are ruled, including voting for their leaders and deciding on laws.

dynasty A line of rulers from the same family.

empire A group of countries ruled by one country that has conquered them.

geometry A branch of mathematics that deals with points, lines, angles and solids.

Golden Age The period of time from around 480 BCE to around 330 BCE, when Greek culture thrived, and great art, literature, philosophy and drama were produced. This time is also known as the 'Classical period'.

Industrial Revolution The period beginning in the late 18th century, when steam power changed the world by improving transport and the way goods were made.

pankration A violent sport that was part wrestling, part boxing. It was an event in the Olympic Games.

Persia A country in south-western Asia that is now Iran.

phalanx A military formation in which Greek soldiers fought in a closely packed rectangular block with their shields touching.

pi The ratio of a circle's circumference to its diameter, approximately equal to 3.14 and shown using the symbol π. The circumference (C) of a circle equals π multiplied by the diameter (D) $-C = \pi D$.

province An area under the control of another country.

siege tower A tower mounted on wheels, which could be moved close to enemy fortifications.

strait A narrow channel of water connecting two larger bodies of water.

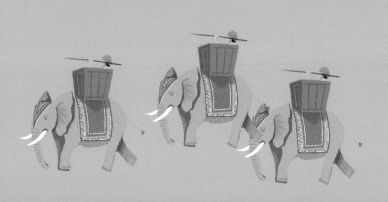

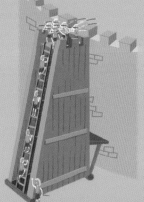

Battles and sieges

... in 30 seconds

Greek soldiers were feared throughout the ancient world as ferocious warriors. That's because they were skilled and experienced. In Sparta, child soldiers trained from the age of seven and all men fought in the army. In Athens, from about 330 BCE, all male citizens were conscripted into the army at 18, and remained on a military list from the ages of 20 to 50.

A few Greek warriors fought on horseback, but most were foot soldiers called hoplites. The hoplites had to buy their own weapons and armour. This was expensive, but it often saved their lives. The poorest citizens couldn't afford all this kit. They just had a bow and arrow, a club or a slingshot with stones, and no armour for protection.

During battles, the armies charged at each other and fought hand to hand with their swords, spears and clubs. Sometimes, an attacking army besieged a city. The soldiers surrounded it to stop anyone going in and out, so people ran out of food. Then they smashed through the walls using catapults and battering rams, entered the city and killed the people inside.

3-second sum-up

In most battles, armies of foot soldiers charged at each other.

3-minute mission Write a coded message

You need: Long strip of paper • Two identical bamboo canes or similar • Pen • Friend

In about 400 BCE, Spartans sent secret messages about their battle plans on strips of paper. They wound the strip around a wooden rod and wrote the message from top to bottom. After unwinding the strip, they filled the gaps with random letters. If enemies seized the message, they couldn't read it. When it reached the intended person, he or she wound the paper around a similar wooden rod to read the message. Try it yourself. Can your friend read the message?

Most Greek soldiers were foot soldiers called hoplites.

Bronze helmet with a crest on top to make the soldier look more impressive

Hoplites had to pay for their own armour and weapons.

Breastplate made from metal or cloth

Long spear for thrusting at the enemy

Short iron sword for stabbing

Round shield, usually decorated with the symbol of the soldier's city or family

Greaves (bronze leg guards)

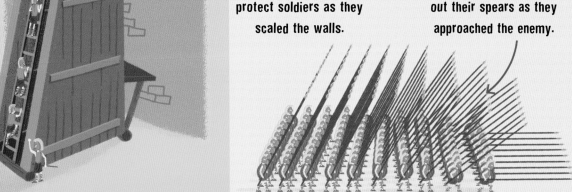

When they attacked enemy cities, the Greeks used siege towers to protect soldiers as they scaled the walls.

In battles, hoplites fought in a dense block called a phalanx. The soldiers at the front held out their spears as they approached the enemy.

Ancient Greece at war

... in 30 seconds

The Golden Age of Greece was punctuated by conflict.
Sometimes the city-states banded together to fight external
enemies, and sometimes they fought each other.

In 490 and 480–479 BCE, the Greek states battled with Persia. In 490 BCE,
the Persian King Darius I attacked the Greeks at the Battle of Marathon.
Despite being outnumbered by two to one, the Greek phalanx stayed solid
and, amazingly, the Greeks won.

The Persian King Xerxes led another assault in 480 BCE, and burnt Athens
to the ground. But the Greeks defeated him at the Battle of Salamis,
the biggest sea battle of ancient times. The following year, they expelled
the last Persian forces from the mainland, and Athens was rebuilt.

The Greek city-states, led by Athens, formed an alliance in 479 BCE called
the Delian League, to stop any future Persian invasion. But some Greek
city-states were angry about Athens' dominance of the League. Sparta
formed the rival Peloponnesian League, and in 431 BCE the two sides went
to war. The Peloponnesian War lasted for years. Athens had a better navy
but Sparta had a stronger army, which led to a long stalemate. In 404 BCE,
Athens finally gave in. But Athens' fall led to the decline of Ancient Greece.

3-second sum-up

Major Greek wars
included the
struggle against
Persia and the
Peloponnesian War.

The Battle of Thermopylae

At the famous Battle of Thermopylae in 480 BCE, a Greek army of just
6,000 men, led by 300 Spartans, held back a 100,000-strong Persian
army at a narrow pass, preventing them from entering Greece. On the
third day, a Greek traitor led the Persians along a secret path so they
could attack the Greek army from the rear. Although the brave
Spartans fought to the death, they were finally overwhelmed.

1. After confronting the Persian army in the open sea, the Greek fleet pretended to retreat, and withdrew to a narrow strait near Salamis. The Persians thought they had given up and followed them, but they had been tricked.

The Greeks defeated a much larger Persian fleet at the Battle of Salamis in 480 BCE.

2. The Greeks forced a battle on the Persians in the strait, where the Persians could not take advantage of their larger fleet. The Greek ambush sunk hundreds of Persian ships.

Greek navy day before battle
Greek navy on day of battle
Persian navy day before battle
Persian navy on day of battle

Athens

Salamis

The Greek and Persian warships were called triremes. They had three rows of oars on each side, powered by 170 oarsmen. The oars and sails allowed them to move fast.

During the battle, Greek ships came alongside the Persian vessels, ramming the sides with their sharp metal prows. The archers fired on their enemies.

Alexander the Great

... in 30 seconds

By the 300s BCE, Greek power was fading. In 338 BCE, Phillip II of Macedonia, in northern Greece, defeated the city-states at the Battle of Chaeronea and brought Greece under Macedonian control. He put an end to Greek democracy but admired Greek culture. Two years later, he was assassinated by one of his bodyguards, and his 20-year-old son Alexander became ruler of the Macedonian Empire.

Alexander

King Alexander was a highly successful general and extremely ambitious. In 334 BCE, he embarked on a campaign of conquest and, over 11 years, he created the biggest empire of the ancient world. He conquered Persia, Syria, Egypt and Afghanistan and spread Greek civilization and culture to these countries. But it still wasn't enough for him.

Alexander the Great began to march through India in 326 BCE. His powerful forces won the Battle of the Hydaspes against a force of 'living tanks' – warriors riding elephants. But Alexander's soldiers were fed up. Most of them had been fighting for eight years and they refused to go further, so the great conqueror retreated.

In 323 BCE, King Alexander was taken ill and died, aged just 33. Yet even after his death, Greek culture was retained in all the countries he had conquered.

3-second sum-up

Alexander the Great created the largest empire of the ancient world.

3-minute mission
King Alexander's death – disease or murder?

To this day, historians disagree over the cause of Alexander the Great's death. Many believe he died of an illness such as malaria, but some think he was poisoned by his generals. Go online and explore some of the different theories. Which do you think is the most likely explanation for his death?

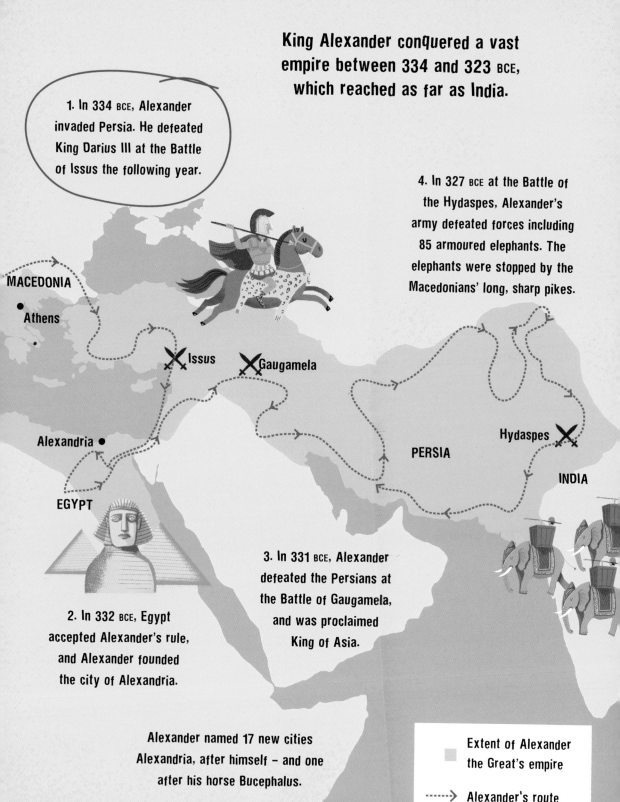

King Alexander conquered a vast empire between 334 and 323 BCE, which reached as far as India.

1. In 334 BCE, Alexander invaded Persia. He defeated King Darius III at the Battle of Issus the following year.

4. In 327 BCE at the Battle of the Hydaspes, Alexander's army defeated forces including 85 armoured elephants. The elephants were stopped by the Macedonians' long, sharp pikes.

MACEDONIA

Athens

Issus

Gaugamela

Alexandria

Hydaspes

PERSIA

INDIA

EGYPT

3. In 331 BCE, Alexander defeated the Persians at the Battle of Gaugamela, and was proclaimed King of Asia.

2. In 332 BCE, Egypt accepted Alexander's rule, and Alexander founded the city of Alexandria.

Alexander named 17 new cities Alexandria, after himself – and one after his horse Bucephalus.

Extent of Alexander the Great's empire

Alexander's route

The Hellenistic age

... in 30 seconds

After Alexander's death, in-fighting broke out as his generals battled to create kingdoms for themselves. Although the Golden Age of Ancient Greece had ended, this era became known as the Hellenistic age. It lasted until 30 BCE.

By 281 BCE, Alexander's empire was divided into three parts, ruled by different dynasties. The Antigonids ruled Greece and Macedonia; the Seleucids were in charge of Asia, Asia Minor and Palestine; and the Ptolemies controlled Egypt.

Yet Greek language and culture continued to spread in western Asia – more widely than ever before. Greece itself was no longer the hub of Hellenism though. The Egyptian city of Alexandria had become a more important economic and cultural centre.

Further west, a new empire was arising. The Romans began to conquer the Hellenistic kingdoms, and in the 100s BCE, Greece became a province of the Roman Empire. Cleopatra was the last Hellenistic ruler of Egypt before the Romans overcame the country in 30 BCE. But the Romans didn't ditch Greek culture. Instead, they adopted Greek ways, keeping alive Greek writing, arts, science, maths and philosophy and transmitting them across their empire.

3-second sum-up

The Hellenistic age lasted until 30 BCE, when the Romans took over the final Hellenistic kingdom.

3-minute mission Match the gods

Many Roman gods were similar to Greek ones. Can you match the Roman names to the original Greek ones? Go online for help.

Greek Zeus, Hera, Ares, Demeter, Poseidon, Hades, Athena, Aphrodite

Roman Juno, Neptune, Minerva, Mars, Venus, Pluto, Ceres, Jupiter

Answers on page 96

323 BCE: Death of Alexander. His generals split up the empire between them and fought among themselves.

After the Golden Age came the Hellenistic age (323–30 BCE), which lasted until the Romans took over.

ANTIGONIDS

Athens

SELEUCIDS

Alexandria

PTOLEMIES

By 281 BCE: The former Macedonian Empire was ruled by three different dynasties: the Antigonids in Greece; the Seleucids in Asia; and the Ptolemies in Egypt.

By around 230 BCE: Alexandria replaced Athens as the centre of learning and science.

The Lighthouse of Alexandria was one of the Seven Wonders of the ancient world.

146 BCE: The Romans invaded, and Greece became a province of the Roman empire.

30 BCE: Egypt fell to Rome.

What did the Greeks do for us?

... in 30 seconds

You may be surprised how much of Greek science and culture is still with us – from maths and medicine to art, architecture, sport, theatre and politics.

Some ideas were well ahead of their time. The principle of democracy did not spread until more than 2,000 years afterwards. In most countries today, citizens can vote for their government. A Greek worked out the principles behind the steam engine 1,700 years before its invention helped kick-start the Industrial Revolution.

Every time you do geometry in class, you're using Greek discoveries. New doctors still swear a modern version of the Hippocratic Oath to promise to keep patients from harm. They advise us to eat well, keep clean and exercise, just as Hippocrates did (see page 34).

In many cities, you'll see buildings inspired by Ancient Greek designs – we call it neo-classical, or 'new' classical architecture. Many theatres and concert halls are modelled on the horseshoe shape of Ancient Greek theatres. All spectators get a great view of the action and can hear what's going on. We read Greek legends, and Greek plays are performed at the theatre.

3-second sum-up

Ancient Greek science and culture still influence the world today.

The Olympic Games

The Romans abolished the Olympics Games around 400 CE. In the late 19th century, the idea of an international sports competition was revived, and the first modern Olympic Games were held in Athens in 1896. The Games have been held every four years since – except during the two world wars. Fortunately, the modern Games don't include dangerous chariot racing or the vicious sport of pankration!

Ancient Greek culture influences architecture, science and political life in modern times.

Greek architecture has inspired many neo-classical buildings such as the Capitol building in Washington, D.C., USA.

We still use many of the Greeks' mathematical ideas today, such as the value of pi.

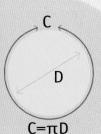

C

D

$C = \pi D$

BALLOT PAPER

Democracy was invented in the early 500s BCE in Athens.

Modern doctors swear a version of the 2,400-year-old Hippocratic Oath.

The first Olympic Games were held in Ancient Greece in 776 BCE.

Many European languages have words that come from Greek.

*anti
auto
hyper
micro*

The Greeks invented the idea of plays performed by actors.

Discover more

NON-FICTION BOOKS

Ancient Greece (Eyewitness), DK, 2014

Ancient Greece (The Best and Worst Jobs) by Clive Gifford, Wayland, 2016

Ancient Greek Adventure by Angela Royston, A&C Black Publishers Ltd, 2010

The Art Book for Children, Phaidon, 2005

Groovy Greeks by Terry Deary, Scholastic, 2016

The History Detective Investigates: Ancient Greece by Rachel Minay, Wayland, 2015

A Visitor's Guide to Ancient Greece by Lesley Sims, Usborne Publishing Ltd, 2015

You Wouldn't Want to Be a Slave in Ancient Greece! by Fiona Macdonald, Book House, 2014

FICTION BOOKS

Aesop's Fables by Aesop, Macmillan, 2017

D'Aulaires' Books of Greek Myths by Ingri d'Aulaire, Delacorte Books for Young Readers, 2017

The Iliad and *The Odyssey* by Gillian Cross, Walker Books, 2015

Treasury of Greek Mythology: Classic Stories of Gods, Goddesses, Heroes & Monsters by Donna Jo Napoli, National Geographic Kids, 2011

You Choose: Ancient Greek Myths by Blake Hoena and Jessica Gunderson, Raintree, 2017

DVDS

Ancient Greece: The Greatest Show on Earth, BBC, 2017

Groovy Greeks, Scholastic, 2005

WEBSITES

Ancient Greece
http://greece.mrdonn.org
Links to pages on many aspects
of Ancient Greek life.

Ancient Greece for Kids
https://ducksters.com/history/
ancient_greece.php
Information on daily life, arts and
culture, mythology and religion.

10 Facts about Ancient Greece
https://www.natgeokids.com/uk/
discover/history/greece/10-facts-
about-the-ancient-greeks/
Facts, photos and links to
information about myths
and religion.

British Museum
http://www.ancientgreece.co.uk
Information about daily life,
festivals, religion, education and
warfare.

'Build a temple' challenge
http://www.ancientgreece.co.uk/
acropolis/challenge/cha_set.html
Follow the instructions to design
a Greek temple.

Although every endeavour has been
made by the publisher to ensure that
all content from these websites is
educational material of the highest
quality and is age appropriate, we
strongly advise that Internet access
is supervised by a responsible adult.

Index

Index

Answers:
Page 88 Match the gods

Zeus = Jupiter; Hera = Juno; Ares = Mars; Demeter = Ceres; Poseidon = Neptune; Hades = Pluto; Athena = Minerva; Aphrodite = Venus.